AF483773

Girl to Girl, Unfiltered

*A collection of stories and photos
discussing self-image and mental health*

ALIQUE TUFENKJIAN

PASADENA, CALIFORNIA

Alique Tufenkjian
1630 San Pasqual Street
Pasadena, CA 91106

Book Layout © 2017 BookDesignTemplates.com

Girl to Girl, Unfiltered/ Alique Tufenkjian. -- 1st ed.
ISBN 979-8-218-15156-0

Contents

Introduction

Girl to Girl, Unfiltered is a collection of honest experiences and stories from eleven teenage girls on the topic of body image and mental health. Alongside photos, they open up about their struggles regarding self-image in hopes of benefitting other girls who may be dealing with similar hardships.

The goal of this book is to show teenage girls that they are not alone in their self-image struggles, and that the "perfect picture" that they see of influencers on social media is not always the truth. As a result of what we see in the media, we tend to scrutinize every part of ourselves in an effort to attain a "perfect" image.

What I want girls to take away from this book are the tools to be empowered in their authentic selves, and to remember that only you have the power to determine your worth—and that is not something measured by your weight, your skin tone, the amount of body hair you have, or any other superficial aspect that you have been made to believe is not good enough.

Do not feel alone; others are going through the same exact thing as you. Use this to uplift each other, and together we can combat the negativity we consume online and all around us.

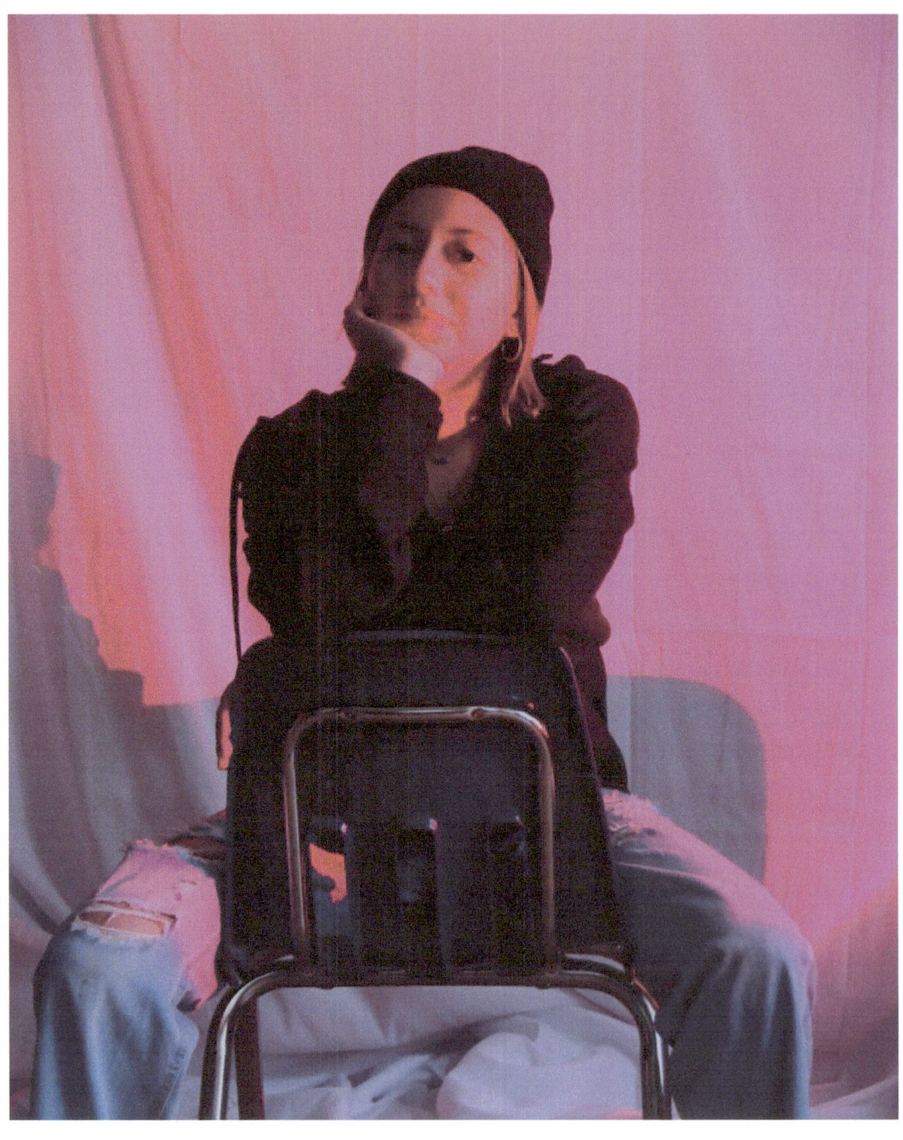

Alique Tufenkjian

1

Giselle

Self-love has never come easy to me. My family, a band of Mexicans who don't even know what self love means (seriously, I don't even know its translation into Spanish), never knew how to show me that I was worthy of love. My parents have struggled with low self esteem their entire lives, and, as a byproduct, I do too. I grew up with parents constantly on diets and weighing themselves. This wasn't their fault—as kids, they were always called chubby or overweight. But what it did teach me was that there was probably something wrong with me, too. Liking myself was never anything really thought about for most of my life. Once I became a teenager, I realized that I wished I was someone else. I wished that I looked differently or had another voice. I wished my nose was smaller, my cheeks less chubby. I wished I was skinnier, and that boys would like me more. For the longest time, I looked in the mirror and wished I would be someone else.

It wasn't until I started learning how to fully be myself that I began to love myself. By this, I mean I discovered a style I loved. I found clothes that hugged my skin in ways I adored, that felt like a layer of protection instead of a burden. I grew into my loves and passions—writing, researching, listening to music. It wasn't until junior year that I began to realize that self-love wasn't an expression of loving yourself because everyone else loves you, but loving yourself because you couldn't imagine living without the things that make you you. While I still struggle with accepting myself and loving who I am, I have stepped into a different life than the one I had as a young teenager. I can dress, feel, and express myself in ways I hadn't before. It was all about taking the plunge and realizing I couldn't be anyone else, so I might as well embrace who I was already.

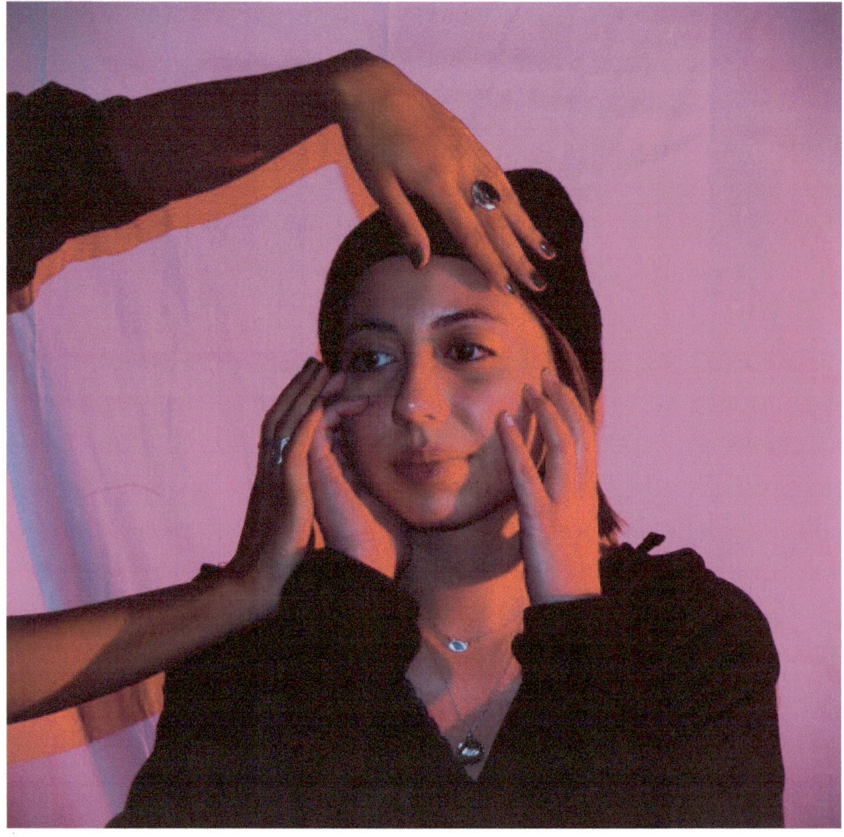

2

Anonymous

I care about my appearance. You could say everyone does on some level, but I have no friends that actually admit to it, making me insecure. I absolutely love to get dressed up, with the makeup, the clothes, the hair, the whole scene. Even just going to school, I like to look nice. I get asked why I put effort in in the morning, and I'll usually just say, "oh, because I had the time." But really, it's because I function better when I like the way I look. If my hair is bothering me one day, then I am going to be in a bad mood and will refuse to do things because of fear of how I am perceived by others. I don't dress for the male gaze, I dress for the entire public gaze.

As shameful as it is, this partly stems from my parents. "Suck in your gut." A phrase repeated to me countless times. I would come downstairs excited to tell my parents something, but before the thought left my mouth, those four words hit me. Suddenly my interest in telling them whatever it was had disappeared. Or, we'd be walking to a restaurant and that phrase plus, "stand up straight," would come at me. When I was little, I never had an eating disorder, but I did strive to be thin. I couldn't fathom not playing a sport or exercising in any way. I thought people wouldn't like me if I didn't fit the beauty standard. And there was some truth behind this. I really found it easier to make friends when I looked nice. If this was because I was more open around people when I allowed them to see me, or if they really did reach out to the nicer looking girls, I won't know.

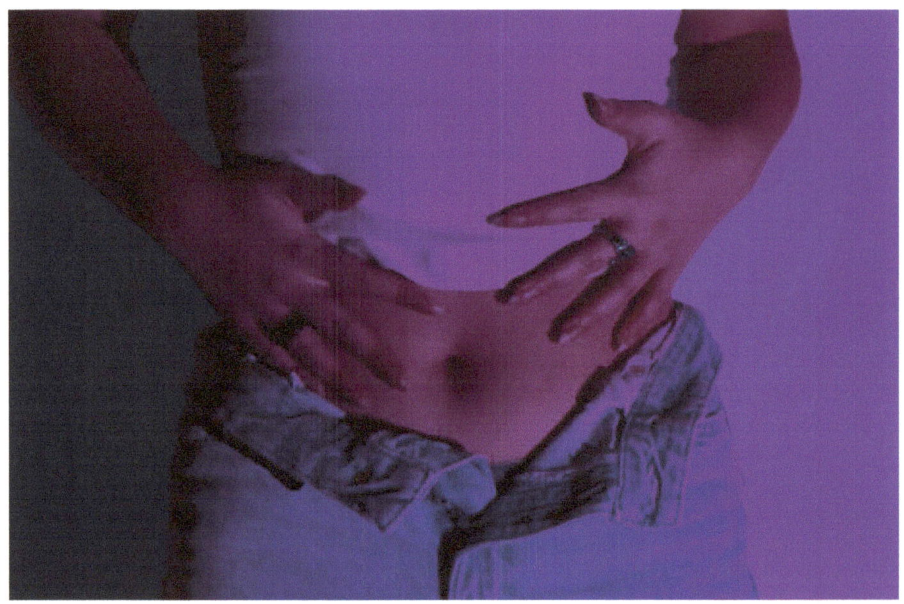

During my junior year, something happened and my mental health took a turn for the worse. I won't get into it, but my anxiety skyrocketed and there were periods when I couldn't eat. Anytime a little bit of anxiety rushed into me, my appetite was gone. I lost 10 pounds which was wild to me, because for the most part I stayed a constant weight for three years. I'm much better now, a year later, but those moments still occur in rarities. I remain with the mentality that I have to eat to survive and feel better, but I definitely don't eat as much as I used to. Anytime I eat something unhealthy, even if it is not enough to change me, I have this sinking feeling in my chest. If there are periods when I don't have a home-cooked meal, I get super down feeling like I'm gaining weight and won't fit into my clothes the way I want to.

But the beauty standard changes. By the time you feel like you fit in, a new fad transpires and your work is gone. But what can you do? Self-love is so amazing, and positive body image makes me happy, but the truth is, there will always be a beauty standard. Everyone is always working towards a goal. Whether it's bettering yourself to fit-in, or working to not change your current state. I wish I could convince myself that I'm perfect the way I am, but someone's always there judging. If there was a solution to accepting yourself and not caring for others' opinions, I'd love to be enlightened.

Alique Tufenkjian

3

Megan

Describe a time you wanted to change something about yourself, and why. Have you ever felt not good enough in any aspect, or somehow less than, in relation to people you've seen on TV/social media?

A feature that I used to want to change about myself was my skin tone. While growing up my grandparents would try to keep me out of the sun to try not to be "too dark." They would always try to make sure I had a hat on and suggested I wear long sleeves to keep my arms from being tan.

Seeing most Asian people in the media today, they have light pale skin, and being Southeast Asian I didn't have pale skin like they did. I thought I wasn't pretty enough to fit the Asian beauty standard that social media brought because I was darker. It made me self-aware of how dark I was and I would compare myself to others. I didn't really try to change my skin tone, but I just didn't feel as pretty as other Asian people who had paler skin.

Growing up I realized that being "darker" than the beauty standard was okay. Not everyone is going to fit the beauty standard and having confidence in yourself is all you really need.

4

Ida

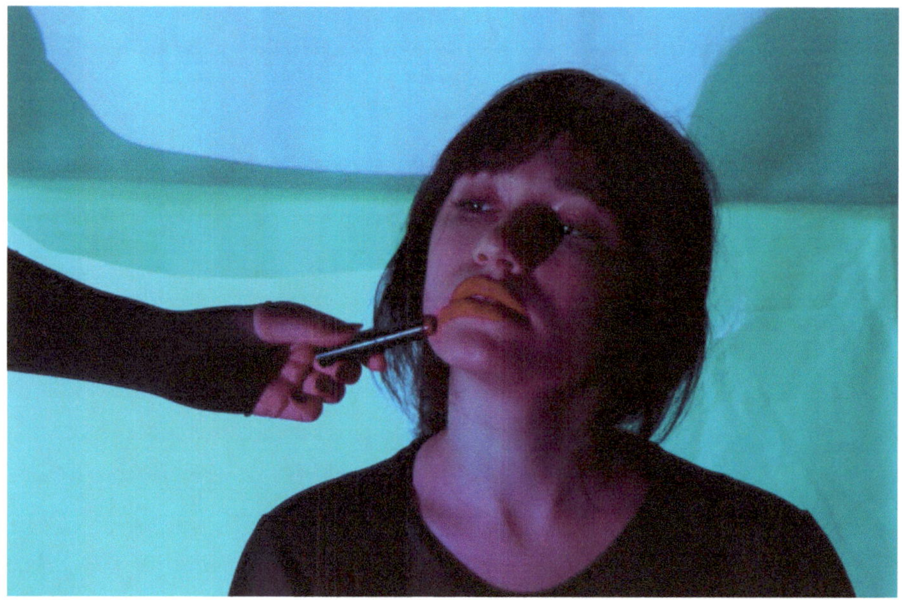

"Like A Painted Picture" – Poem by Ida Hartel

She's like a painted picture
Something so beautiful
Something so captivating
Recognize the strokes of paint in every line and detail
She is like a painted picture
Yet she has been painted over so many times
Changed and fixed to look "Perfect"
"Painted to perfection" they say
Painted over until satisfied
Covered up and controlled
She has become this visual for others to see
Left with little to no identity besides looks
Painted with an unremovable smile
For she has no choice
The paint has already dried
She must pretend
"She can just pretend" they say
That she's always looked this way
Always Felt this way
Always Been seen this way
It can't be that hard
It hurts her
But it can't hurt
For she's perfect
So why would it hurt?
After all,
She is like a painted picture.

5

Trinity

I don't think there has ever been a time in my life when I have been completely satisfied with who I am. I'm the type of person that always strives for the best; it doesn't make sense to me to not do something to the best of my abilities. I struggle with this quality of mine, because while holding myself to a high standard can be a good thing, I often find myself using it as a way to degrade myself. I'm always looking for something I can do better and I'm never satisfied.

It took me a long time to admit to myself that I look for validation whether that be male validation, academic validation, or anything else that validates the self-improvement that I'm always working on. While academic validation is one of my main worries, I find that my body has always been an issue on my mind. My struggle with my body image has been such a long-standing issue and it's gotten to the point where it's just normal. Being unsatisfied with the way I look is normal. I'm curvy in both the right and wrong places and if my lips were a little bit bigger or my waist a little smaller or my jawline a little more defined maybe I'd be satisfied.

But even after all those things I could still also have smaller arms and thighs and thicker eyelashes. Whenever I look in the mirror there is always something about my body that I could fix, that could always be better, and maybe then I'll get that small ounce of validation that I strive for, recognizing my efforts, and encouraging me to continue to fix things.

I find both comfort and sadness knowing that so many people, specifically young women, are right alongside me with our relationship with our bodies. My journey to being completely satisfied is by no means over and I don't think it ever will be, but I do think trying my best at loving myself is all I can do, even if it's really hard sometimes.

6

Elle

2/28/2022 – Journal entry: My experience w/ mental health

Probably the first time I experienced a change in my mental health is when I joined gymnastics. I remember getting frustrated during practice, and my coach asked me what was wrong and I said "I don't know." Then she asked, "Are you frustrated?" and I said yes, even though I didn't even know what that word meant. During my gym career is where I really started to grow my mental health issues—I had a ton of mental blocks, aka fear, doubt, hesitation. On vault, I'd run down the runway and stop at the board, over and over again, even though I just had a great vault the day before. I wasn't sure what was wrong with me. It wasn't fear. To this day, I still don't know what it is. I had similar mental blocks on every event; floor, beam, and bars. Some because of fear, and some because, as I said, I don't know.

I also started having body image issues during that time. I was this muscular, swoll, 4'10 - 4'11 little Filipino girl. I hated my buff arms, but also accepted them because everyone else admired them. I also disliked my wide ribs, and I still do to this day. I also have a confession to make. On my last, final day of my whole gymnastics career, I finished it off with a mental block. It still haunts me to this day. Filled with guilt, hatred, and regret. Now that my gymnastics career has ended, the only mental health issue I suffer from is body image. After I quit gym, I've definitely gained weight, lost my visible abs, and added more roundness to my face. I'm also confused, because I like my arms because they look strong, yet I don't like how they look muscular. That's where I'm stuck currently. This body image issue peaked over quarantine. I'd do the basic cry myself to sleep routine. Sometimes I'd think of not eating, but I know that'll lead to even more issues. I fortunately don't suffer from depression and anxiety, which I'm super grateful for. Therefore, I've learned to accept my emotions, grow from them, and love just the way I am.

7

Maddie

Hey! My name is Madeline Stukel, but everyone calls me Maddie. I hold a lot of big leadership positions at my school, and was voted most popular in our senior class! I am the overall Secretary in ASB as well as Jewish club president, Science National Honors Society Vice President, varsity softball captain for two years now, and am the baseball team's head manager. I have also played numerous sports such as basketball, volleyball, and wrestling, before settling into four years of varsity softball. I have gotten mostly A's throughout high school, and readily take all the AP classes my school offers which have recently resulted in a 4.84 weighted GPA.

The reason all of this bragging is a part of my story is because I only recently realized how amazing that all looked on the outside. In other words, how amazing it looked when I only mentioned the good stuff, the things I told the colleges I am applying to. I only shared with you what makes me look great, in words that make me sound even better.

But, in reality, my high school life was a much larger struggle.

I was combating countless mental health issues (like ADHD, generalized anxiety and panic disorder, and depression), many of which were ignored by the people closest to me. I have overcome a majority of the conflicts of mental health, but I still to this day struggle with it all. Among the long list of things I have been diagnosed with, body dysmorphia and generalized eating disorder were two of the most difficult things I had to overcome.

My "good days" and "bad days" were mostly dependent on my mood and however bloated or hungry I was, but at the time I thought I was either "fat" or "skinny." My skinny days felt amazing! I could wear a tight shirt, and low-waisted jeans, and feel good about myself when I looked in the mirror. However, this just made my bad days so much worse. I would wear hoodies in 95° weather, with high-waisted jeans or sweatpants. I would feel extremely hungry and just stare inside the fridge for around five minutes until I decided I wasn't hungry. I would get mad at myself for wanting to eat anything that wasn't a plain piece of lettuce. All I consumed was coffee in the morning, and a big snack when I got home from school. I would convince myself I wasn't hungry for dinner, but then was so hungry right before bed I would eat any snack foods I could find. Chips, crackers, dry cereal, nothing was safe. After my late-night snacks, I would feel so ashamed for eating that much "disgusting" food, thinking I should have just eaten a small portion of dinner, and cry myself to sleep out of shame.

I would wake up in the morning, and the cycle would start all over again.

I was always envying the 25-year-old Instagram models with paper-thin waists and big butts and breasts that were nearly impossible to achieve without surgery. How could they be that skinny and that happy at the same time?

This kept up for a few months, well into softball season, and I was actually glad that I lost some weight and looked skinnier. But I knew it wasn't right. I wasn't actually happy or healthy. I had no energy anymore. I was losing sleep and valuable nutrition that came with actual meals. I had lost so much energy that my body didn't even bother making me hungry anymore, I would just get into a really bad mood. I was beginning to get mean to the people around me and had a short temper. I would also doze off in class, and to prevent myself from doing so, I would dig my nails into the skin on the back of my other hand, so much so there would be marks there for the rest of the day.

I was confused, and frustrated, and came to a realization that I needed to get better. I recognized that nobody was going to help me unless I wanted to help myself. I made the decision to get the body that made me happy. I ate healthier, more regular meals, and was able to show up to practice with as much energy as I needed to succeed and get a good amount of exercise. My mental health was doing better, and because of that, I understood that whatever body I had at the moment, was the body that made me happy.

It took me a long time to realize that, like all of the bragging I did to you (and my colleges) about my high school years, Instagram models only brag about their good days. They don't post when their hair is greasy up in a messy bun because they haven't showered in three days. Why would they post in a regular t-shirt and sweatpants when they have a much sexier outfit in the closet that will gain thousands of more likes? They cover pimples and blemishes before taking a picture. They hold their stomach in and smile for the one second the picture is taken, because it only takes a second. No matter what they are feeling, nobody ever really posts the "ugly" facts.

Anyone on social media, including my friends, including me, gets to pick and choose what the world sees of them. I'm not posting a picture laying in bed with my greasy hair, acne, and hoodie that has spaghetti and ice cream stains on it. I'm looking through my camera roll, posting pictures that I took at the beach with my friends a month ago, which we prepared and posed for hours for.

Everyone's happy days are something to cherish, no matter who you are or what that looks like for you. But, at the same time, everyone's yucky days should be valued just as much, if not more. We need those days to reflect and remind ourselves to appreciate the days when we feel happy. I have found so much joy and contentment in every single day, ever since I began recognizing that the yuck was necessary. I now am even happier on happy days, and feel at peace on yuck days, not upset, ashamed, or disgusted like I used to be, but rather grateful for my body which I get to call perfect, no matter what kind of day I'm having, because whatever body Maddie is in, is perfect; and the same goes for you.

8

Anonymous

Describe a time when you wanted to change something about yourself and why.

A time where I wanted to change something about myself was during the summer. I wanted to change how my stomach looks. After seeing every day on social media girls who have super flat stomachs or abs, I wanted to look like those girls. I wanted to be comfortable in a bikini. I felt super insecure about not meeting that beauty standard that it made me feel less than.

Is there anything that's helped you love your authentic self more?

One thing that has helped me love my authentic self more was hanging out with the right people.

In my early years of high school, I had a group of friends that would text, FaceTime and hangout a bunch. But as my time in high school progressed, I soon found out that they weren't my true friends. Time after time some of these friends would constantly make me get left out of plans, put down, made fun of, and I started feeling ignored by my so called "friends" and it really affected me mentally. I would often cry wondering what I was doing wrong, or why I deserved this, as I always tried my best to be kind to them. I soon realized that real friends wouldn't do this as friends are supposed to support you, care for you and love you for who you are. You don't need to change for certain people to like you. After I realized that the friends I was hanging out with weren't making me feel good, I turned to find people who appreciated me. I found people who made me realize the value of friendship again and I am truly grateful for that. Having a group of friends who love you and make you feel good are the best. This has made me love my authentic self more because of my real, true friends.

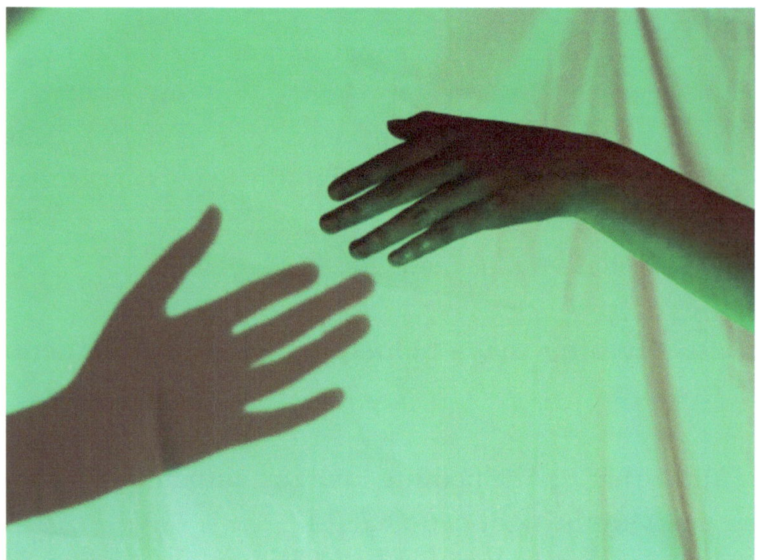

9

Anonymous

Have you ever felt not good enough in any aspect, or somehow less than, in relation to people you've seen on TV/social media?

Of course. The media we consume has created these false expectations of we, as women, should be. Paired with the immaturity and lack of education of younger generations, it really causes a lot of harm to so many young and impressionable girls, like who I once was.

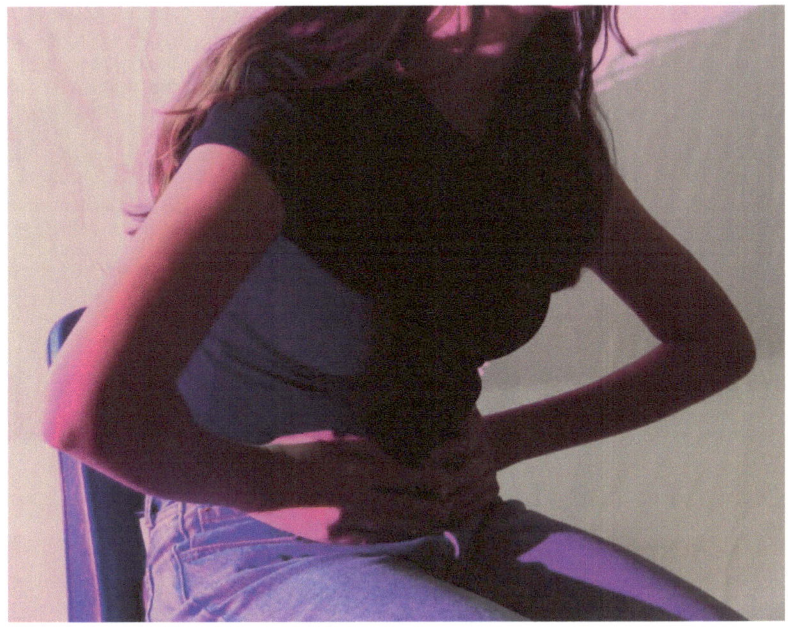

Has the media ever made you aware of something about your looks that you didn't realize was a "problem" before?

I've always seen insecurity trends come and go. It's like a new insecurity is being cranked out every day. Hip dips, buccal fat, cankles, noses, lip shape, the most random and odd things you can think of, but I've never let it bother me. I've been made aware I may have some of those features, but I've never been insecure about it because most of those things are natural, normal, and beautiful.

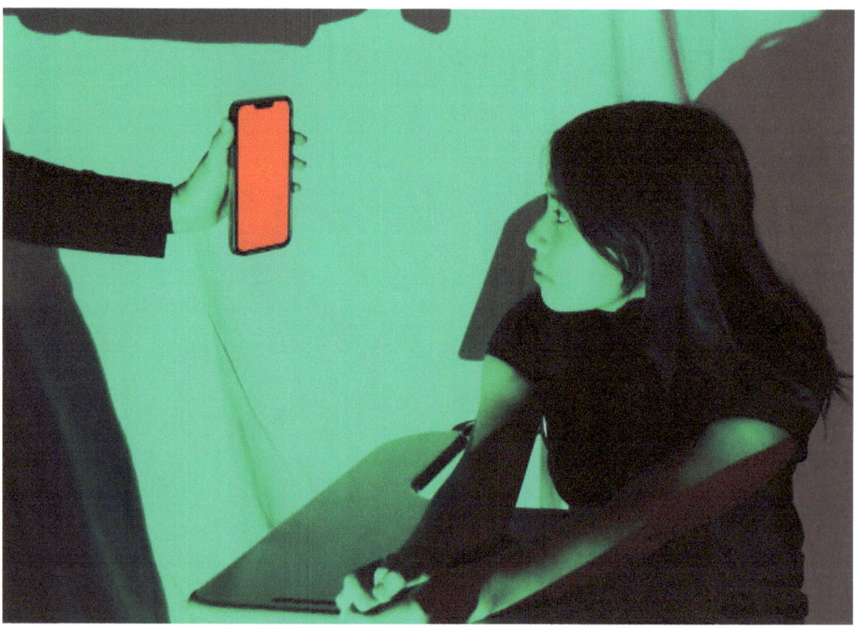

Describe a time when you wanted to change something about yourself, and why.

As a person whose ethnicity tends to have more hair, I always hated my hair. Arm hair, leg hair, bushy eyebrows, mustache. All of it. I wanted to get rid of it all. Why? Because I was under the impression that it was weird. It's not. It's really not. Hair is natural and it's there for a reason. WARMTH!

Is there anything that's helped you love your authentic self more? (Hanging out with friends, spending less time on social media, not comparing yourself to others, listening to music, etc.)

Finding friends with similar ethnic backgrounds and relating over not being part of a certain standard of beauty really helped me grow and appreciate my features. My eyebrows, my skin tone, my hair, all of it. Listening to our folk music, eating our food, and practicing our traditions have made me so proud to be who I am and look the way I do.

Would you say you're done with your self-love/identity journey? And are you completely comfortable with who you are, or is it a journey you're still taking (if any journey at all)?

Of course not. As much as I love myself more, there's ALWAYS room for more love. Endless amounts of love. I am more than comfortable with who I am. I love who I am, the person I've become. I've experienced so many things, and I've always been there for myself, no matter what. I'm my best friend. And I can control the person I am and always improve. To infinity.

Describe a time someone made you feel inferior because of a superficial trait and how that has affected you. How did you overcome it if at all?

Someone once pointed out my arm hair in middle school. He said I had more arm hair than him. I laughed at him. In that moment, I was confused. Was this really happening?? Yes, it was. But I realized he was the one acting, to put it nicely, asinine. He made himself look ignorant and shallow.

What's something that you'd want other teenage/preteen girls to know regarding battling the beauty standard and loving their authentic selves?

I want every young girl to know the truth. The world is harsh. It is miserable. But it is your choice how you live in it. You either succumb to the ignorance and buffoonery, or you conquer it and live your life to the fullest. You are powerful. It is in YOUR hands. Do not be helpless.

10

Anonymous

Femininity is something that I've always felt out of touch with.

For all of my life, I've been socialized as a woman, but I've never truly felt like one. I've always felt as if my features were too masculine for me to be a woman, yet remained too feminine for me to ever be considered a man. Growing up, I never perceived myself entirely as female, as I failed to relate to the conventional definition of a woman.

I lacked the sweet and nurturing nature that's supposed to accompany a woman. My demeanor was mostly cold, uninviting, and almost intimidating. I was uncomfortable with the idea of intimacy—both physical and emotional. Affection hadn't been an innate ability of mine, and I instead had to learn it. I didn't have the delicate, thin figure nor the grace of a woman. My chest was flat, my arms were heavy, and my calves were robust (of larger size than a man's). My voice was also deeper than that of my male acquaintances. It felt as if every aspect about me didn't align with what a woman was.

Even now, at the age of eighteen, my disconnection with femininity prevails. Though I've realized that being a woman is not confined to such a traditional image, my perspective on myself remains dictated by these views.

11

Alyson

I have always been insecure of the amount of body hair I have. The way women are depicted in films typically show a slender, blue eye beauty with no body hair. Unlike the women on screen, I had visible body hair on my arms and legs. I hadn't really thought much about it until middle school. All the girls in my grade had smooth legs and arms. Not only did this make me more aware of how I looked but it made me want to change how I looked. Around this time, I also began to get social media. I became obsessed with trying to fit the standards that surround me in the media and at school. As I grew, I realized that I wasn't the only person who had felt this way and that there were others who felt the same way as me. Together, we helped each other embrace our insecurities to build a better environment.

WE
EW

Acknowledgements

Thank you to the eleven girls I worked with for sharing your personal stories with me for this project, and for contributing your time to the photoshoots! I appreciate your commitment and your willingness to be open. All of your stories are truly meaningful and relatable.

Also, I'd like to thank my advisors Mandy Denaux and Chelsea Byers for their valuable guidance on this project.

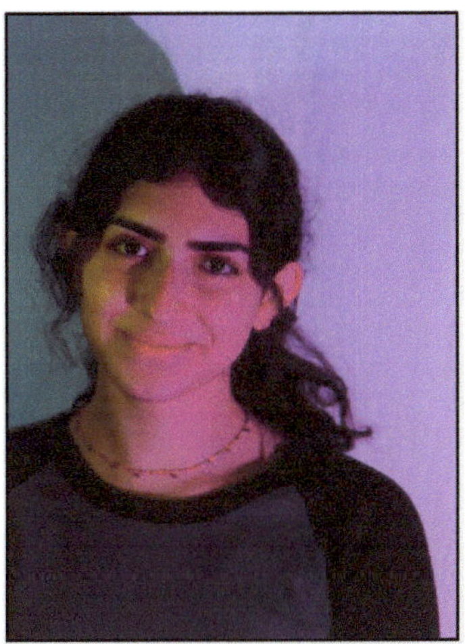

Alique saw a common issue amongst teen girls—how the media had a negative impact on their mental health and self-image. She came to the realization that almost everyone around her was silently going through the same thing, and she wondered why it was not discussed more. She sought a way to let other teenage girls know that they are not alone in the struggles they face in regards to self-image. To carry out her idea, she used photography as a medium for change.

She gathered a team of eleven girls, all with unique stories. Utilizing her love of photography, she conducted photoshoots of each of the girls. She then asked them questions on the topic of body image, mental health, and beauty standards, which elicited a degree of candid vulnerability from her participants.

Gathering their short stories to fit together in one larger picture—like pieces of a puzzle—she recognized more clearly than ever that almost all girls go through similar things, but hardly anyone ever talks about it with each other.

She hopes that through this project, other teenage girls will become more open to having these "unfiltered" discussions with each other. She wants girls to feel less alone in what they are facing, and more empowered in their authentic selves.

www.ingramcontent.com/pod-product-compliance
Lightning Source LLC
Chambersburg PA
CBHW040521120726
48010CB00005B/203